Scotland
A CELEBRATION

Scotland
A CELEBRATION

MERCAT PRESS
EDINBURGH

The photographers (the numbers refer to the pages on which their pictures appear):
Paul Adair 125; Alan and Heather Barnes 75, 86(l); Dennis Barnes 17, 35, 39, 126, 128(l); Angus Blackburn 9;
Dorothy Burrows 99; Jack Byers 21; Laurie Campbell i, ii-iii, vi, 10, 11, 81(r), 114-115; Ray Chaplin 80; Brian Chapple 123;
John G. Corbett 79, 97; Andrea Cringean 146; Penny Davies 6; Richard Elliot 63, 66(l), 69, 112(r);
Alister Firth 16, 20, 22, 23, 24, 27, 31, 66(r); Alan Gordon 73, 82, 101; John Guidi 25, 28, 29, 32, 132; Doug Houghton 94-95, 98, 125;
Angus Johnston 33, 62, 84; Bob Lawson 4, 18-19, 96, 142; Genevieve Leaper 44; Gordon Lockie 7; Vincent Lowe 90, 92, 127;
John MacPherson 46-47, 53, 56, 57, 58, 78, 87; Don McKinnell 57, 150; Ian McLean 30; Susan McMillan 41, 50(r), 77;
Roberto Matassa 26, 48, 49, 52, 55, 58, 59, 60, 61, 81(l), 86(r), 88, 89, 91, 116, 136-137; Matt Miller 119, 130-131;
Ellice Milton 104, 106; Martin Moar 3, 140, 145, 149, 151; Bill Robertson 93, 111, 129, 133, 134, 141; C.K. Robeson 1, 2, 5, 143;
Glynn Satterley 38, 64, 71, 76, 83, 102, 105, 120, 122, 152; Richard Schofield 68, 70, 107, 113; Phil Seale 40; David Tarn 12-13, 14, 15;
James Weir 34, 100, 103; Ronald Weir 36, 37, 42-43, 44, 45, 50(l), 51, 54, 56, 65, 67, 72, 74, 85, 108-109, 110, 112(l), 117,
118, 121, 124, 128(r), 135, 148; Curtis Welsh 138-139; John Wilkinson 8, 144, 147.

First published in 1999 by
Mercat Press
James Thin,
53 South Bridge,
Edinburgh EH1 1YS

ISBN: 1873644922

All pictures sourced through
Scotland in Focus
Ladhope Vale House,
Galashiels,
Selkirkshire TD1 1BT

Design: Mark Blackadder

Printed in Hong Kong through World Print Ltd

IV

CONTENTS

VI

SCOTS PINE

SCOTLAND, A CELEBRATION

In the following pages Scotland, in all its beauty and variety, is celebrated in pictures. In an attempt to capture the essential character of Scotland and its ever-changing aspects in all seasons and weathers, the work of some of the finest contemporary photographers in the country has been collected together.

Their pictures celebrate the wonderful diversity and drama of a landscape which is imbued with history. Every scene has a tale to tell. The hills, glens and moors of Scotland are covered with the relics of the past, from the prehistoric stone circles of Orkney to the abandoned cottages of St Kilda. Each sturdy keep or tumbled ruin has witnessed a vivid pageant of joy or sorrow, triumph or tragedy. Castles in their day may have played a dramatic part in Border warfare or in the Jacobite uprising; now their ruins are as much a part of the landscape as the cliffs on which they stand. Elsewhere, churches express in stone the piety of former days, while harbour-walls defiantly recall the unceasing struggle to wrest a living from the stormy waters of the open sea beyond.

This is not, however, a nostalgic or backward-looking collection. These pictures also celebrate the rich diversity of the present. For sheer scenic beauty Scotland remains unsurpassed, attracting a friendly invasion every year by visitors from around the world. The towns and cities whose colourful annals have been described by the great Scots writers continue to be vibrant and dynamic. For its scientific and industrial achievements Dundee has been dubbed 'the City of Discovery'. Edinburgh is 'the Festival City', its many annual arts festivals going from strength to strength. Meanwhile, Glasgow's busy commercial centre is thriving and its museums and galleries, both old and new, contribute to a lively cultural scene.

The pictures point to the future as well. They reflect a new mood of national pride and self-confidence among Scots that has sometimes been lacking in previous years. The establishment of the new Scottish Parliament in Edinburgh marks a transformation of Scottish life. It has created a feeling that Scotland, a nation once again, can go forward into the twenty-first century with optimism. There will, of course, be squalls and stormy seas ahead. But as the new millennium begins, and fireworks burst in the skies above Edinburgh and Glasgow, there is so much in Scotland and Scottish life to celebrate.

VII

THE BORDERS

2

PREVIOUS PAGE. THE CHEVIOT HILLS, WHICH MARK THE BORDER BETWEEN ENGLAND AND SCOTLAND.
THESE LONELY FIELDS HAVE SEEN MANY AN ARMY OR RAIDING PARTY STEAL BY IN THE CHILLY LIGHT OF DAWN

LEFT. A PICTURE TAKEN FROM THE POINT ABOVE ABBOTSFORD, 'SCOTT S VIEW', WHERE THE GREAT NOVELIST
SIR WALTER SCOTT WOULD OFTEN SIT AND LOOK OUT OVER HIS BELOVED EILDON HILLS AND BORDER VALLEYS.

RIGHT. THE ANNUAL SELKIRK COMMON RIDING CELEBRATES THE HEROISM OF THE 100 SELKIRK MEN WHO FOUGHT
AT THE BATTLE OF FLODDEN. ONLY ONE RETURNED ALIVE TO THE TOWN, CARRYING A CAPTURED BANNER.

3

MELROSE ABBEY, FOUNDED IN THE TWELFTH CENTURY AND REBUILT IN THE FIFTEENTH CENTURY,
FROM WHEN THESE STATELY RUINS DATE. HERE, IN A LEAD CASKET, IS BURIED THE HEART OF ROBERT THE BRUCE.

5

HAUNTED SMAILHOLM TOWER IN ROXBURGHSHIRE, WHERE A SPECTRAL KNIGHT IS SOMETIMES SEEN. SIR WALTER SCOTT GREW UP NEARBY, AND TOLD THE GHOSTLY TALE IN HIS BALLAD *The Eve of St John*.

6

A RAINY DAY AT KELSO ON THE RIVER TWEED. THE TOWN GREW UP BY A FORD ON THE RIVER. NEARBY ARE FLOORS CASTLE AND THE RUINS OF THE MEDIEVAL KELSO ABBEY.

TRAQUAIR HOUSE, INNERLEITHEN, HOSTS A CRAFT AND MUSIC FAIR EVERY AUGUST. AS WELL AS ENJOYING PERFORMERS LIKE
THESE ENGLISH MORRIS DANCERS, VISITORS CAN SAMPLE THE TRAQUAIR ALE, WHICH IS MADE ON THE PREMISES.

8

FIELDS OF OILSEED RAPE NEAR KELSO MAKE A VIBRANT SPECTACLE. THIS CROP IS A RECENT INTRODUCTION TO SCOTTISH AGRICULTURE. DISLIKED BY SOME, ITS COLOUR AND SCENT CANNOT BE IGNORED!

SHEEPDOG TRIALS AT PEEBLES, WHERE THE SKILL OF BOTH SHEPHERD AND DOG ARE TESTED. THE LOCAL ECONOMY STILL
DEPENDS HEAVILY ON THE ASSOCIATED INDUSTRIES OF SHEEP-FARMING AND WEAVING.

TWO ASPECTS OF THE TWEED AS A FAMOUS SALMON RIVER. ABOVE, WE SEE A SPORTSMAN PREPARING TO CAST HIS FLY. OPPOSITE,
WE SEE COMMERCIAL FISHERMEN SPREADING NETS FOR SALMON IN THE WIDE EXPANSE
OF WATER WHERE THE TWEED MEETS THE SEA.

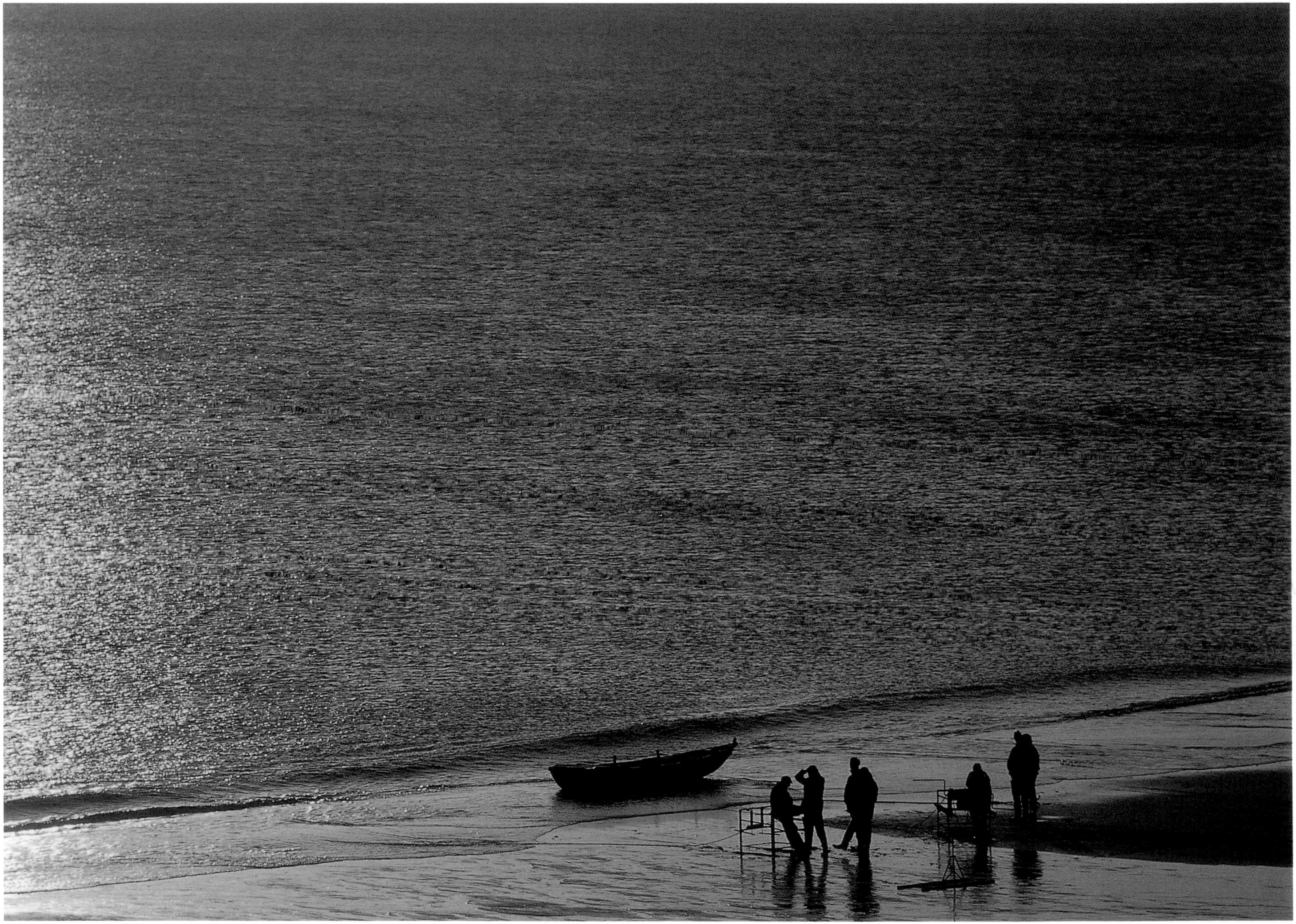

THE SOUTH WEST

THE ANCIENT MOATED CAERLAVEROCK CASTLE NEAR DUMFRIES. ITS HISTORY MATCHES ITS DRAMATIC APPEARANCE.
BESIEGED BY EDWARD I IN 1300, ARMIES FROM EITHER SIDE OF THE BORDER HAVE FOUGHT OVER IT SINCE.

PREVIOUS PAGE. THE SPECTACULAR COASTLINE AT ST ABBS, BERWICKSHIRE, WHERE 300-FOOT HIGH CLIFFS ARE HOME TO
ONE OF SCOTLAND S LARGEST SEABIRD COLONIES. A LIGHTHOUSE ALERTS SEAFARERS TO THE TREACHEROUS ROCKS BELOW.

SWEETHEART ABBEY, ALSO KNOWN AS NEW ABBEY, WAS FOUNDED IN 1273 BY DEVORGUILLA, WIDOW OF JOHN BALLIOL, IN HIS MEMORY. WHEN SHE DIED, SHE HAD HIS 'SWEET HEART' BURIED WITH HER.

THE CAMERA OBSCURA IN DUMFRIES WAS CONSTRUCTED IN 1836 ON THE TOP LEVEL OF A CONVERTED WINDMILL.

INSIDE, ON A CLEAR DAY, A PANORAMIC VIEW OF DUMFRIES IS PROJECTED ONTO A TABLE-TOP SCREEN.

NOT A SCENE FROM SOUTHERN FRANCE BUT A GARDEN IN SOUTH WEST SCOTLAND! THE EXOTIC PLANTS AND TREES OF
LOGAN BOTANIC GARDENS ARE MADE POSSIBLE BY THE MILD INFLUENCE OF THE GULF STREAM.

THE BROODING WALLS OF DUNURE CASTLE, WITH AILSA CRAIG IN THE BACKGROUND. IN THE CASTLE'S BLACK VAULTS THE UNSCRUPULOUS EARL OF CASSILLIS ONCE ROASTED A LOCAL LAIRD OVER A FIRE TO EXTORT HIS LANDS FROM HIM.

PREVIOUS PAGE. WITH ITS FINE HARBOUR, SEEN HERE, AND WIDE SANDY BEACHES, GIRVAN HAS LONG BEEN A POPULAR HOLIDAY DESTINATION FOR GLASGOW PEOPLE. LESS BUSY IN RECENT YEARS, IT STILL HAS MANY ATTRACTIONS.

CULZEAN CASTLE, AYRSHIRE, BUILT BY THE GREAT SCOTTISH ARCHITECT ROBERT ADAM. A FLAT IN THE CASTLE WAS GIFTED TO GENERAL EISENHOWER FOR HIS HELP TO THE ALLIES DURING THE SECOND WORLD WAR.

THE MONUMENT IN ALLOWAY TO AYRSHIRE'S FAVOURITE SON, ROBERT 'RABBIE' BURNS. BORN INTO POVERTY, THE PLOUGHMAN POET BECAME ONE OF THE BEST–LOVED OF ALL WRITERS,
HIS WORKS NOW FAMOUS THROUGHOUT THE WORLD.

THE COTTAGE WHERE ROBERT BURNS WAS BORN ON 25 JANUARY, 1759. THIS DATE IS NOW CELEBRATED EVERY YEAR BY BURNS' NIGHT SUPPERS, DURING WHICH HIS *Ode to a Haggis* IS SOLEMNLY RECITED.

AYR AND THE NEW BRIG OVER THE RIVER AYR, BY NIGHT. 'AULD AYR, WHAM NE'ER A TOWN SURPASSES, FOR HONEST MEN AND BONNY LASSES', WROTE BURNS. LONG MAY THIS DESCRIPTION REMAIN TRUE!

RIGHT. GLASGOW UNIVERSITY IN WINTER. FOUNDED IN 1451 BY BISHOP WILLIAM TURNBULL, IT NOW CENTRES ON THIS MAGNIFICENT NEO-GOTHIC BUILDING. BUILT IN 1887-91, IT DOMINATES THE CITY SKYLINE.

26

TWO VIEWS OF GEORGE SQUARE IN GLASGOW. ITS WIDE OPEN SPACES ARE A FOCAL POINT AND MEETING PLACE AMID THE BUSY GLASGOW STREETS. IN SUMMER IT IS THRONGED WITH SHOPPERS AND TOURISTS.

27

AT CHRISTMAS TIME THE SHOPPERS ARE JOINED BY CAROL-SINGERS, BRASS BANDS AND A
GIANT CHRISTMAS TREE—AND REVELLERS OF EVERY AGE AND DESCRIPTION.

GLASGOW'S STATUS AS A VENUE FOR IMPORTANT INTERNATIONAL CONFERENCES IS ENHANCED BY THE
NEWLY-BUILT ARMADILLO CENTRE. ITS APTLY-NAMED AUDITORIUM BY THE RIVER CLYDE
CAN ACCOMMODATE 3,000 DELEGATES.

THE MAGNIFICENT KIBBLE PALACE IN GLASGOW BOTANIC GARDENS. BUILT BY ENGINEER JOHN KIBBLE, IT WAS PRESENTED TO THE ROYAL BOTANIC INSTITUTION WHICH FOUNDED THE GARDENS IN 1881.
IT NOW HOUSES TEMPERATE FLORA.

THE GLASGOW GALLERY OF MODERN ART (GOMA) WAS OPENED IN 1996 AMID MUCH CONTROVERSY ABOUT THE QUALITY OF
THE EXHIBITS. THE BERYL COOK PICTURES, SEEN HERE, WERE AMONG THE MOST HOTLY DEBATED.

THE WILLOW TEA ROOMS ON SAUCHIEHALL STREET IN GLASGOW, CREATED BY THE FAMOUS ARTIST AND ARCHITECT CHARLES RENNIE MACKINTOSH.
THE DESIGN SUGGESTS A WILLOW GROVE, THE ORIGINAL MEANING OF SAUCHIEHALL.

32

LEFT. THE MITCHELL LIBRARY, GLASGOW. FOUNDED IN 1877 AS THE RESULT OF A BEQUEST, AND MOVED TO ITS PRESENT BUILDING IN 1911, IT IS SCOTLAND'S LARGEST LIBRARY OPEN TO THE GENERAL PUBLIC.

GLASGOW MOSQUE, ONE OF MANY MOSQUES IN SCOTLAND. SCOTLAND IS NOW HOME TO PEOPLE OF MANY ETHNIC BACKGROUNDS
AND TRADITIONS, AND THE ISLAMIC COMMUNITY PLAYS A PROMINENT PART IN SCOTTISH LIFE.

THE 'BONNY, BONNY BANKS' AND CLEAR BLUE WATERS OF LOCH LOMOND SEEN FROM LUSS,
WITH BEN LOMOND, THE 'BEACON HILL', RISING IN THE BACKGROUND.

THE TROSSACHS, THE COUNTRY BETWEEN CALLANDER AND LOCH LOMOND, CONTAIN SOME OF THE MOST ROMANTIC SCENERY IN SCOTLAND. THIS IS MACGREGOR COUNTRY, ONCE THE STRONGHOLD OF THE FAMOUS OUTLAW, ROB ROY.

36

A VIEW OF LOCH AND BEN LOMOND FROM INVERUGLAS, NEAR KINGUSSIE. LOCH LOMOND, THE LARGEST EXPANSE OF FRESH WATER IN BRITAIN,
ACTS AS THE DOMESTIC AND INDUSTRIAL WATER-SUPPLY FOR MUCH OF CENTRAL SCOTLAND.

ONE OF THE MOST ROMANTIC OF ALL SCOTTISH CASTLES, THE FIFTEENTH-CENTURY KILCHURN CASTLE ON LOCH AWE. GARRISONED DURING THE 1745 UPRISING, IT WAS DAMAGED BY LIGHTNING SHORTLY AFTERWARDS AND BECAME DISUSED.

38

LEFT. FRUITS OF THE SEA AT LOCH ETIVE MUSSEL FARM.
SCOTTISH SHELLFISH ARE EXPORTED ROUND THE WORLD, TO EUROPE AND
THE FAR EAST IN PARTICULAR. HERE MUSSELS ARE BEING GROWN ON A THICK ROPE.

RIGHT. OBAN, KNOWN AS THE CHARING CROSS OF THE HIGHLANDS BECAUSE IT IS THE
MEETING-POINT OF ROAD, RAIL AND FERRY ROUTES. MCCAIG S TOWER,
ON THE HILL, IS AN UNFINISHED MODEL OF THE COLOSSEUM.

40

JUST OFF THE WEST COAST, THE ISLE OF ARRAN IS A LITTLE GEM OF SCENIC BEAUTY, WITH CRAGS IN THE NORTH AND GENTLER SCENERY TO THE SOUTH. GOAT FELL, SHOWN HERE, IS THE ISLAND S HIGHEST POINT.

SUNSET OVER LAGGAN BAY, ISLAY. THIS BEAUTIFUL ISLAND WAS ONCE THE STRONGHOLD OF THE LORDS
OF THE ISLES. NOW IT IS FAMOUS FOR THE CLASSIC MALT WHISKIES PRODUCED HERE.

OVERLEAF. THE UNMISTAKABLE BRIGHTLY PAINTED HOUSES OF TOBERMORY IN MULL. CREATED AS A FISHING PORT
IN THE EIGHTEENTH CENTURY, IT NOW PROVIDES A WELCOMING HARBOUR FOR YACHTS AND PLEASURE BOATS.

42

44

ONE OF MANY BREATHTAKING VIEWS ON THE ISLE OF MULL. THIS ISLAND, FOR ALL ITS DESERTED
LANDSCAPES, IS STEEPED IN HISTORY, AND ARCHAEOLOGICAL REMAINS FROM THE BRONZE
AGE ONWARDS CAN BE FOUND HERE.

NEAR TO MULL IS FINGAL'S CAVE ON THE ISLE OF STAFFA. THIS EXTRAORDINARY PLACE, FORMED
FROM HEXAGONAL BASALT COLUMNS, HAS BEEN CELEBRATED IN POETRY, ART AND MUSIC—
NOTABLY IN MENDELSSOHN'S OVERTURE.

ST MARTIN'S CROSS IN IONA SYMBOLISES THE RICH HERITAGE OF CELTIC CHRISTIANITY ON THIS HOLY ISLAND, WHERE ST COLUMBA FOUNDED HIS RELIGIOUS COMMUNITY IN 563 AD, AND WHERE 48 SCOTTISH KINGS ARE BURIED.

HIGHLANDS AND ISLANDS

48

THE MASSIVE CONE OF BUACHAILLE ETIVE MÒR, 'THE BIG HERDSMAN OF ETIVE', RISES DRAMATICALLY FROM THE TAWNY LEVELS OF RANNOCH MOOR.
ITS INSTANTLY RECOGNISABLE OUTLINE IS A LANDMARK FOR CLIMBERS AND WALKERS.

AUTUMN IN GLEN ETIVE WHERE, ACCORDING TO THE ANCIENT LEGENDS, DEIRDRE ROAMED THE HILLS WITH HER DOOMED
LOVER NAOISE, HUNTING THE RED DEER. LATER, THE LOCH WOULD ECHO TO HER LAMENT FOR HIM.

PREVIOUS PAGE. ONE OF THE MOST ROMANTIC SIGHTS IN THE HIGHLANDS, A RED DEER HERD ON THE HILL AS NIGHT
BEGINS TO FALL. INDIGENOUS TO SCOTLAND, RED DEER ROAM THE HIGHLAND GLENS IN LARGE NUMBERS.

THE WILD BEAUTY OF THE PASS OF GLENCOE. AT TIMES, DESPITE ITS LOVELINESS, IT HAS A DARK AND FORBIDDING ASPECT, ITS HISTORY STAINED INDELIBLY BY THE MASSACRE IN 1692 OF THE MACDONALDS IN THE GLEN BY COMPANIES OF THE EARL OF ARGYLE'S REGIMENT.

A SKIER ON AENACH MOR IN THE NEVIS RANGE. WINTER SPORTS ARE POPULAR IN THE HIGHLANDS, BUT RECENT MILD WINTERS HAVE RESTRICTED THE SEASON TO A FEW WEEKS IN THE YEAR.

52

A WINTRY SCENE NEAR DALWHINNIE. THE HIGHLANDS IN WINTER, THOUGH AT TIMES ROADS BECOME BLOCKED AND POWER-LINES ARE BROUGHT DOWN BY SNOW, HAVE A UNIQUE BEAUTY OF THEIR OWN.

A CROFTER TENDS TO A YOUNG HIGHLAND COW, THE FAMILIAR SHAPE OF BEN NEVIS IN THE BACKGROUND. CROFTING—
SMALL-SCALE SUBSISTENCE FARMING—IS STILL A VIABLE, THOUGH ARDUOUS, WAY OF LIFE IN THE HIGHLANDS.

54

THE CALEDONIAN CANAL WITH BEN NEVIS IN THE DISTANCE. OPENED IN 1822, THIS CANAL IS THE LONGEST IN
SCOTLAND, RUNNING EAST TO WEST THROUGH LOCH LOCHY, LOCH OICH AND LOCH NESS.

55

LOCH EILT—LOCH OF THE HIND, OR YOUNG DEER. NEAR HERE IS THE TRUNK OF A GREAT OAK TREE WHERE BONNIE PRINCE CHARLIE SHELTERED DURING HIS WANDERINGS AFTER THE FATAL BATTLE OF CULLODEN.

CUTTING PEAT AT ARDNAMURCHAN. ONCE AN ESSENTIAL
PART OF DOMESTIC LIFE IN THE HIGHLANDS, PEAT-CUTTING BY HAND IS
NOW QUITE RARE, THOUGH IT IS CARRIED OUT ON AN INDUSTRIAL SCALE IN SOME AREAS.

CORPACH, IN THE LEE OF BEN NEVIS. AT CORPACH, 'THE PLACE OF THE BODIES', GALLEYS ONCE
WAITED TO CARRY DEAD KINGS AND NOBLES DOWN LOCH LINNHE FOR BURIAL
IN THE HOLY ISLAND OF IONA.

SUNRISE GRADUALLY DISPERSES THE MISTS OVER LOCH AILORT. THIS SHELTERED
SEA LOCH OPENS OUT INTO THE SOUND OF ARISAIG, EMBRACING THE ARDNISH PENINSULA.

57

THIS STEAM TRAIN AT LOCHAILORT IS ON THE WEST HIGHLAND LINE BETWEEN FORT WILLIAM
AND MALLAIG, ONE OF THE MOST ROMANTIC AND PICTURESQUE JOURNEYS IN EUROPE.
THERE IS STILL A REGULAR STEAM TRAIN SERVICE.

BELOW AND RIGHT. THE BEAUTY OF THE WESTERN ISLANDS VARIES EXQUISITELY AND
INFINITELY WITH THE EVER-CHANGING CONDITIONS AND TIME OF DAY. HERE THE FIRM
OUTLINE OF RUM AND EIGG, SEEN FROM SAME POINT ON LOCH AILORT, IS MAGICALLY TRANSFORMED.

KELP ON THE SHORE AT ARISAIG. AN IDYLLIC SCENE, BUT THIS SEAWEED HAS BITTER ASSOCIATIONS IN
THE HIGHLANDS. MANY CLEARANCES WERE UNDERTAKEN BY LANDLORDS TO PROVIDE
FORCED LABOUR FOR THE KELP-MAKING INDUSTRY.

EILEAN DONAN CASTLE ON ITS ROCKY ISLAND AT THE MOUTH OF LOCH DUICH IS THE MOST PICTURESQUE
OF FORTIFICATIONS. A JACOBITE STRONGHOLD, IT WAS BOMBARDED BY HER MAJESTY'S SHIP
Worcester IN 1719 AND DESTROYED. IT WAS RESTORED TO ITS PRESENT STATE
OF REPAIR DURING THE NINETEENTH CENTURY.

THE JAGGED HORSESHOE-RIDGE OF THE BLACK CUILLINS NEAR SLIGACHAN, SKYE, A DRAMATIC
SKYLINE WHICH HAS LONG BEEN ADMIRED BY POETS AND PAINTERS—
'SUBLIME IN BARRENNESS' AS SCOTT DESCRIBED IT.

NEAR TO THE BLACK CUILLINS ARE THE RED CUILLINS, SEEN HERE. THESE PRESENT A MORE ROUNDED, SOFTER SCENERY, BEING MADE OF A SOFTER ROCK THAN THEIR VOLCANIC NEIGHBOURS.

64

ERISKAY, A TINY ISLAND NEAR BARRA, HAS GIVEN ITS NAME TO A BREED OF PONY, SEEN HERE. ERISKAY PONIES ARE THE ONLY SURVIVING DESCENDANTS
OF THE NATIVE SCOTTISH PONY, WHICH WAS ONCE WIDESPREAD.

KISIMUL CASTLE, JUST OFF THE SHORE AT CASTLEBAY, ISLE OF BARRA. A STRONGHOLD OF THE MACNEILS, IT ENABLED THEM TO HOLD ON TO BARRA DESPITE THE HOSTILITY OF THE LORDS OF THE ISLES.

66

TYPICAL COASTAL CROFT-HOUSES ON NORTH UIST IN THE OUTER HEBRIDES. THE STRAW AND MARRAM THATCH ON THE BUILDINGS IS
WEIGHTED DOWN WITH STONES AS PROTECTION FROM THE FIERCE ATLANTIC GALES.

THE PURE, CLEAR WATER AND LONG SANDY BEACHES OF HARRIS IN THE OUTER HEBRIDES. STRICTLY SPEAKING IT IS NOT AN ISLAND IN ITS OWN RIGHT, SINCE IT IS CONNECTED
TO THE ISLE OF LEWIS BY A SMALL ISTHMUS TO THE NORTH, BUT ITS VERY DIFFERENT MOUNTAINOUS SCENERY GIVES IT ITS OWN UNIQUE CHARACTER.

THE IRON AGE DUN CARLOWAY BROCH ON LEWIS DEMONSTRATES THE IMMENSE ENGINEERING AND ARCHITECTURAL SKILL

OF THE EARLY ISLANDERS. BROCHS LIKE THIS, THOUGH USED AS DWELLING HOUSES, WERE ALSO FORMIDABLE FORTS.

TIME STANDS STILL WITHIN THE CIRCLE OF CALLANISH STANDING STONES ON THE ISLE OF LEWIS. RELICS OF THE BRONZE AGE, THESE ANCIENT STONES CONVEY A DEEP SENSE OF SPIRITUAL POWER.

PORT OF NESS ON THE NORTH-EAST COAST OF THE ISLE OF LEWIS. THE SMALL HARBOUR HERE PROVIDES
A STURDY SHELTER FROM THE ATLANTIC BREAKERS THAT ROAR IN FROM THE DEEP OCEAN.

71

THE JUDGES COMPARE NOTES DURING A TRADITIONAL HIGHLAND GAMES. HELD THROUGHOUT THE REGION, THESE GAMES FEATURE COMPETITIONS RANGING FROM FIELD SPORTS
TO HIGHLAND DANCING. THE PARTICIPANTS TAKE THE RAIN IN THEIR STRIDE!

BEN MORE COIGACH STANDS LIKE AN ISLAND IN A SEA OF MIST. THE COIGACH IS A REMOTE UPLAND AREA IN ROSS
AND CROMARTY, WHERE THE INVERPOLLY NATURE RESERVE HAS RECENTLY BEEN ESTABLISHED.

ULLAPOOL HARBOUR, WESTER ROSS. FOUNDED AS A PORT IN 1788 BY THE BRITISH FISHERIES SOCIETY, ULLAPOOL HAS REMAINED
A FOCUS OF FISHING ACTIVITY IN THE WEST, AS WELL AS A CENTRE OF TOURISM.

THE MOUNTAIN OF CUL MÒR, SUTHERLAND, IS THE LARGEST OF COIGACH'S PEAKS. FROM ITS SUMMIT PLATEAU THERE ARE BREATHTAKING VIEWS OF THE SURROUNDING COUNTRY OF COIGACH AND ASSYNT.

BEYOND THE CALM WATERS OF CAM LOCH LIES THE UNMISTAKABLE BULK OF SUILVEN, LIKE A BEACHED WHALE. A FAVOURITE MOUNTAIN OF THE POET NORMAN MACCAIG, IT DOMINATES THE SURROUNDING LANDSCAPE.

A DARK GEMSTONE IN A SILVER SETTING, ARDVRECK CASTLE ON LOCH ASSYNT WAS BUILT BY THE MACLEODS IN THE THIRTEENTH CENTURY. DESTROYED BY FIRE, IT HAS STOOD AS A DESERTED RUIN FOR TWO CENTURIES.

THE REMOTE LOCHS OF THE FAR NORTH OF SCOTLAND PROVIDE SPORTS FISHING WHICH IS SECOND TO NONE IN EUROPE. HERE A PARTY OF ANGLERS TRY THEIR LUCK ON LOCH STACK IN SUTHERLAND.

THE SECLUSION OF BADCALL BAY, SUTHERLAND. THE LANDSCAPE, BEAUTIFUL THOUGH IT IS, IS HARSH AND
ROCKY, INCAPABLE OF SUPPORTING ANY FORM OF FARMING BEYOND A FEW SHEEP.

78

THE COASTLINE OF NORTH WEST SCOTLAND HAS MANY MOODS. ABOVE, LEFT. TOWARDS EVENING, SANDWOOD BAY IN SUTHERLAND IS MYSTERIOUS, SOLEMN AND SUBDUED.

ABOVE, RIGHT. DAWN ON SANGO BEACH NEAR DURNESS IS FRESH, SERENE AND SMILING.

A STORM RAGES OVER THE KYLE OF TONGUE, AN INLET ON THE CAITHNESS COAST. ON THE CLIFF BELOW THE WALLS OF A VIKING FORT WITHSTAND THE TEMPEST, AS THEY HAVE DONE FOR CENTURIES.

A FEROCIOUS HUNTER, THE SCOTTISH WILDCAT LIVES IN THE WILDEST AND MOST INACCESSIBLE PARTS OF THE HIGHLANDS. RARE AND SECRETIVE,
IT IS NOT OFTEN SEEN—AND STILL LESS OFTEN PHOTOGRAPHED.

A 'MONARCH OF THE GLEN' POSES FOR HIS PORTRAIT. RED DEER LIKE THIS STAG CAN BE SEEN
THROUGHOUT THE HIGHLANDS. ORIGINALLY WOODLAND ANIMALS, THEY
HAVE ADAPTED TO LIFE ON THE BARREN MOORS.

IN THE REMOTE AREAS OF THE HIGHLANDS THERE CAN BE FEW MORE MAJESTIC SIGHTS THAN THE
OUTSTRETCHED WINGS OF THE GOLDEN EAGLE. ONCE HUNTED NEARLY TO
EXTINCTION, ITS NUMBERS ARE NOW RECOVERING.

82

KEISS CASTLE IN CAITHNESS STANDS ON THE VERY EDGE OF A CLIFF OVERLOOKING THE SEA. ERECTED IN THE SIXTEENTH CENTURY,
IT WAS OWNED BY THE SINCLAIR FAMILY, BUT IS NOW RUINOUS AND DESERTED.

'MY HEART'S IN THE HIGHLANDS, A-CHASING THE DEER.' DEER STALKERS IN SUTHERLAND MAKE THEIR WAY BACK FROM THE HILL AFTER A SUCCESSFUL DAY, CARRYING THE DEAD STAG ON A HIGHLAND PONY.

84

LAGGAN HYDRO ELECTRIC DAM.

LOCH LAGGAN AND THE MAMORE MOUNTAINS. DESPITE ITS SERENE BEAUTY, LOCH LAGGAN HAS VERY PRACTICAL USES.
AT THE HEADWATERS OF THE RIVER SPEAN, IT ACTS AS A RESERVOIR OF FRESH WATER AND
SOURCE OF HYDRO–ELECTRIC POWER THROUGH THE LAGGAN DAM.

HIGHLAND CATTLE, WITH THEIR SHAGGY COATS AND RUGGED BUILD, ARE UNIQUELY SUITED TO THE
HARSH CONDITIONS OF THE SCOTTISH HILLS IN WINTER. DESPITE THEIR HARDY
APPEARANCE, THEY PRODUCE BEEF OF SUPERLATIVE QUALITY.

SUNSET OVER LOCH GARRY, ATHOLL. SEEN FROM THIS ANGLE,
THE LOCH'S WELL-KNOWN RESEMBLANCE
TO A MAP OF SCOTLAND IS STRIKING.

RIGHT. THE GLENFINNAN MONUMENT TO THE 1745 UPRISING. THROUGHOUT SCOTLAND, JACOBITES RALLIED TO BONNIE PRINCE CHARLIE WHEN HE
ASSERTED HIS RIGHT TO THE BRITISH THRONE. HIS FORCES WERE FINALLY CRUSHED AT CULLODEN.

88

URQUHART CASTLE ON LOCH NESS. THE SITE WHERE IT STANDS IS STREWN WITH RUINS FROM VARIOUS PERIODS OF HISTORY FROM THE IRON AGE ONWARDS.
THE MAIN BUILDING DATES FROM THE SEVENTEENTH CENTURY.

INVERNESS, THE 'CAPITAL OF THE HIGHLANDS'. AT THE HEAD OF THE GREAT GLEN, INVERNESS IS THE HUB OF ROAD
AND RAIL LINKS AND THE ADMINISTRATIVE CENTRE FOR MUCH OF THE HIGHLAND REGION.

OIL RIGS IN THE CROMARTY FIRTH. THE DISCOVERY IN 1970 OF OIL AND GAS RESERVES
IN THE NORTH SEA HAS HAD A DRAMATIC EFFECT ON SCOTLAND'S ECONOMY,
AND THAT OF BRITAIN AS A WHOLE.

DALWHINNIE WHISKY DISTILLERY, SPEYSIDE. THE MALT WHISKIES PRODUCED IN DISTILLERIES LIKE THIS ALONG THE BANKS OF THE RIVER
SPEY HAVE A DISTINCTIVE FLAVOUR AND QUALITY THAT HAS MADE THEM WORLD FAMOUS.

92

THE LOWER SLOPES OF BRAERIACH, IN THE CAIRNGORMS, WHICH AT OVER 4,000FT IS ONE OF THE HIGHEST PEAKS IN THE RANGE. ALMOST ALL OF THE RANGE IS ABOVE 3,500FT.

LAIRIG GHRU, A DEEP MOUNTAIN PASS, ACCESSIBLE ONLY ON FOOT, DIVIDING THE EAST AND WEST RANGES OF THE CAIRNGORMS. THE WALK THROUGH IT IS ONE OF THE GREAT HIGHLAND ROUTES.

THERE CAN BE NO MORE MAJESTIC AND EXHILARATING SIGHT—AND SOUND!—THAN A PIPE-BAND IN FULL HIGHLAND REGALIA, MARCHING ALONG IN THE OPEN AIR, LIKE THIS ONE AT NETHY BRIDGE.

PREVIOUS PAGE. THE OLD MAN OF HOY, ORKNEY.
A TOWERING SEA STACK, IT STANDS IMPERVIOUS TO THE WAVES BOILING
AROUND ITS FEET. THE CLIFFS BEHIND IT ARE 300 METRES HIGH, AMONG THE HIGHEST IN BRITAIN.

HOY IS THE SECOND-LARGEST OF THE ORKNEY ISLANDS, BATTERED AND WEATHERED BY THE CONSTANT
POUNDING OF THE SEA. IN THE PICTURE ON THE LEFT WE SEE HOY'S CLIFFS AND THE TURMOIL
OF THE WAVES FROM YESNABY ON THE MAINLAND; IN THE PICTURE ABOVE
A DILAPIDATED OLD CROFT-HOUSE ON THE SHORE
AT RACKWICK BAY IN HOY ITSELF.

ORKNEY HAS ONE OF THE LARGEST AND BEST-PRESERVED CONCENTRATIONS OF PREHISTORIC SITES IN
EUROPE, RANGING FROM THE 5,000 YEAR-OLD UNDERGROUND VILLAGE OF SKARA BRAE TO
THE AWESOME MEGALITHIC MONUMENTS, OF THE SAME PERIOD, SHOWN
HERE—THE GREAT RING OF BRODGAR NEXT TO HARRAY LOCH (ABOVE)
AND (RIGHT) THE STENNESS HENGE CLOSE BY.

ITALIAN WORLD WAR II PRISONERS-OF-WAR, USING THE MOST BASIC MATERIALS, CREATED THIS BEAUTIFUL
CHAPEL INSIDE A NISSEN HUT AT LAMB HOLM, ORKNEY. IT REMAINS TODAY
AS A TESTIMONY TO THEIR ARTISTRY AND FAITH.

KIRKWALL HARBOUR, ORKNEY. KIRKWALL IS THE CAPITAL OF ORKNEY AND ITS MAIN PORT, ITS CLUSTER OF BUILDINGS
IN RED STONE HUDDLED ROUND THE MASSIVE TWELFTH-CENTURY CATHEDRAL OF ST MAGNUS.

THE WEST COAST OF FAIR ISLE IN THE SHETLAND ISLANDS. FAMOUS AS A SITE FOR BIRD-WATCHING, IT IS PROBABLY EVEN MORE RENOWNED FOR ITS TRADITION OF KNITTING IN THE DISTINCTIVE FAIR ISLE PATTERNS.

A CROFTER WORKS THE PEAT IN SHETLAND. LIKE MUCH OF THE HIGHLANDS AND THE HEBRIDES, SHETLAND IS ALMOST TREELESS, AND PEAT, CUT IN THE AGE-OLD WAY, REMAINS AN ESSENTIAL DOMESTIC FUEL.

LEFT. SHETLAND PONIES GRAZE CONTENTEDLY IN THE FLOWER-RICH
MEADOWS OF SUMMER. THEIR THICK, SHAGGY COATS AND SHORT, STOCKY BUILD
ARE IDEALLY ADAPTED TO WITHSTAND THE WORST RIGOURS OF THE SHETLAND WINTER.

RIGHT. THE UP-HELLY-AA FIRE FESTIVAL IS HELD EVERY JANUARY IN LERWICK, SHETLAND.
TORCH-BEARING WARRIORS ESCORT A FULL-SIZED VIKING LONG-SHIP IN PROCESSION,
THEN BURN IT AMID RIOTOUS CELEBRATIONS, CASTING THEIR
TORCHES INTO THE BLAZE.

FOLK MUSIC LIVES AND THRIVES THROUGHOUT SCOTLAND, AND SHETLAND IS PARTICULARLY NOTED
FOR ITS FIDDLE-PLAYING TRADITION. HERE THE GREATEST SHETLAND FIDDLER OF
THEM ALL, ALY BAIN, PLAYS WITH PHIL CUNNINGHAM.

THE DESERTED VILLAGE OF HIRTA, ST KILDA. FAR OUT IN THE ATLANTIC, ST KILDA IS A WILD AND BARREN PLACE. BY 1930 THE ISLANDERS' WAY OF LIFE HAD BECOME UNSUSTAINABLE, AND ALL WERE EVACUATED.

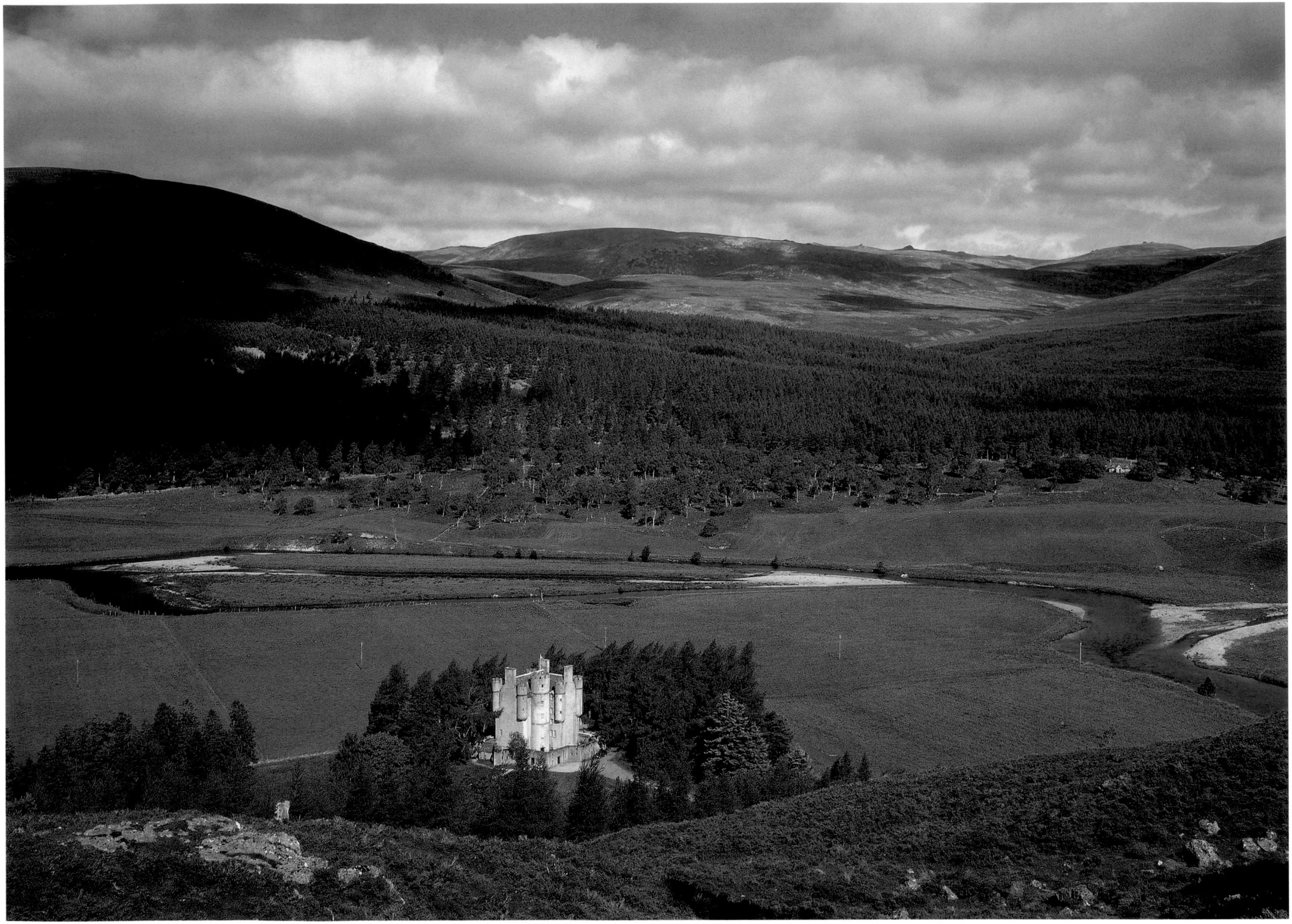

PREVIOUS PAGE. BALMORAL CASTLE, DEESIDE,
THE SUMMER HOLIDAY RESIDENCE OF THE QUEEN AND THE ROYAL FAMILY. IT WAS
BOUGHT BY QUEEN VICTORIA AND PRINCE ALBERT, WHO LOVED ITS SECLUSION AND UNSPOILT CHARM.

LEFT. BRAEMAR CASTLE ON THE BANKS OF THE RIVER DEE. BUILT AS A HUNTING-LODGE BY THE
EARL OF MAR IN 1628, IT BECAME A GARRISON FOR GOVERNMENT FORCES AFTER THE '45 UPRISING.

RIGHT. ELGIN CATHEDRAL IN MORAYSHIRE, SAID TO HAVE BEEN THE MOST BEAUTIFUL IN SCOTLAND.
CONSECRATED IN 1224, IT WAS PARTIALLY DESTROYED BY THE WOLF OF BADENOCH,
THEN REDUCED TO A RUIN AFTER THE REFORMATION.

ABERDEEN, THE GRANITE CITY, REMAINS A GREAT MARITIME PORT. SCOTLAND'S THIRD LARGEST CITY, IT HAS BEEN REVITALISED BY THE NORTH SEA OIL AND GAS BOOM FROM THE SEVENTIES ONWARDS.
FERRIES AND CRUISE SHIPS CALL INTO THE HARBOUR, WHICH IN RECENT YEARS HAS HOSTED THE TALL SHIPS RACE.

112

DUNNOTTAR CASTLE, STONEHAVEN, IS A GROUP OF SEVERAL BUILDINGS ON A CRAGGY HEADLAND ACCESSIBLE ONLY BY A NARROW AND DANGEROUS PATH.
OFTEN BESEIGED, IT WAS USED AS A PRISON DURING THE SEVENTEENTH CENTURY.

PERTHSHIRE AND TAYSIDE

PREVIOUS PAGE. IN THE WINTER, DEER IN THE
HIGHLANDS HAVE ONLY TWO ENEMIES: THE DEER-STALKER, AND THE WEATHER.
HERE A RED DEER STAG SITS OUT A BLIZZARD, ON THIS OCCASION STALKED ONLY BY THE CAMERA.

LEFT AND RIGHT. BLAIR CASTLE IN PERTHSHIRE HAS BEEN, SINCE THE THIRTEENTH CENTURY, THE
FAMILY SEAT OF THE DUKES OF ATHOLL, MANY OF WHOM HAVE PLAYED AN IMPORTANT PART IN
SCOTLAND'S HISTORY. LORD GEORGE MURRAY, FOR EXAMPLE, WAS BONNIE PRINCE CHARLIE'S
MILITARY COMMANDER DURING THE '45 UPRISING. MANY HISTORICAL RELICS IN
THE HOUSE INCLUDE THE COLLECTION OF ARMS IN THE BALLROOM.

118

MIST VEILS THE SURFACE OF LOCH TUMMEL IN PERTHSHIRE. SITUATED IN THE LOVELY TUMMEL
VALLEY, THIS LOCH HAS BEEN DOUBLED IN EXTENT AS A RESULT OF
HYDRO-ELECTRIC WORKS AT ITS EAST END.

PERTHSHIRE IS FAMOUS FOR ITS AUTUMN COLOURS. LARCH, BIRCH AND OAK TREES AT THE EDGE OF
LOCH DUNMORE, PITLOCHRY, FORM AN EXQUISITE PATTERN OF TONES AND TEXTURES.

IN LOCH TAY, THE SOURCE OF THE RIVER TAY, THE REMAINS OF 18 CRANNOGS—PREHISTORIC LAKE DWELLINGS—HAVE BEEN FOUND. A MODERN RECONSTRUCTION SHOWS HOW THEY WOULD HAVE LOOKED.

USUALLY OPEN
9AM - 6PM MONDAY
L SATURDAY ∝ OFTEN
EVENINGS UNTIL 10
RING DOOR BELL
∝ HAUD ON
A MINUTE
(TILL I GET MY BOOTS ON)

120

LEFT. SCOTTISH RIVERS, SUCH AS THE RIVER TAY,
ABOUND IN SALMON, AND SALMON FISHING IS A POPULAR SPORT. MANY SMALL,
LOCAL SMOKEHOUSES PRODUCE SMOKED SALMON OF UNPARALLELED QUALITY AND FLAVOUR.

RIGHT. SPRING FLOWERS NEAR KENMORE WITH BEN LAWERS IN THE DISTANCE. THE WILD
HYACINTHS (BLUEBELLS) THAT CARPET THE GLEN HAVE BEEN DESCRIBED AS
'HEAVEN LOOKING UP FROM THE GROUND'.

THE DRAWING ROOM OF GLAMIS CASTLE, A PLACE FOREVER ASSOCIATED WITH SHAKESPEARE'S *Macbeth*. APPROPRIATELY, IT IS HAUNTED BY THE GHOST OF LADY GLAMIS WHO WAS BURNT AS A WITCH BY JAMES V.

THE HERMITAGE, A FAMOUS BEAUTY SPOT ALONG THE BANKS OF THE RIVER BRAAN REACHED BY A
WOODLAND WALK FROM DUNKELD. A VIEWING PLATFORM OVERLOOKS THE FALLS OF BRAAN.

CAPTAIN SCOTT'S SHIP *Discovery* AT DISCOVERY
POINT, DUNDEE. FAMOUS FOR ITS 'THREE JS', JUTE, JAM AND JOURNALISM,
DUNDEE HAS A PROUD MARITIME AND SHIP-BUILDING HERITAGE. *Discovery* WAS BUILT HERE IN 1901.

PERTH, ON THE RIVER TAY, IS A ROYAL BURGH, A MARKET TOWN AND AN IMPORTANT AGRICULTURAL
CENTRE FOR THE REGION, HOSTING THE PERTHSHIRE AGRICULTURAL SHOW AND
SALES OF ABERDEEN-ANGUS AND HIGHLAND CATTLE.

THE NAME OF ST ANDREWS IS ASSOCIATED
THROUGHOUT THE WORLD WITH THE ROYAL AND ANCIENT GOLF CLUB
AND THE OLD COURSE. THE 'HOME OF GOLF' STILL REGULARLY HOSTS MAJOR TOURNAMENTS.

THE REMAINS OF ST ANDREWS CATHEDRAL REFLECT THE CITY'S IMPORTANCE IN RELIGIOUS, POLITICAL
AND EDUCATIONAL HISTORY. FOR CENTURIES THE CENTRE OF THE SCOTTISH CHURCH,
IT IS ALSO THE HOME OF SCOTLAND'S FIRST UNIVERSITY.

THE PICTURESQUE HARBOUR OF CRAIL IN THE EAST NEUK OF FIFE. THE EAST NEUK IS A STRETCH OF COASTLINE ALONG WHICH
SEVERAL LITTLE SEA-PORTS AND FISHING VILLAGES ARE FOUND. THEY REMAIN LARGELY UNSPOILT.

BEINN DORAIN IN THE BREADALBANE HILLS. THIS BEAUTIFUL AND SCENIC AREA WAS ONCE IN THE
POSSESSION OF THE EARLS OF BREADALBANE, BUT WITHIN THE LAST TWO
CENTURIES OWNERSHIP HAS BECOME FRAGMENTED.

BEINN CHEATHAICH IN GLEN DOCHART, CLAD IN THE RUSSET OF AUTUMN. THESE HILLS WERE ONCE THE HAUNT OF THE OUTLAW ROB ROY MACGREGOR: HE AND HIS WIFE ARE BURIED IN NEARBY BALQUHIDDER KIRKYARD.

LOCH LUBNAIG IN THE TROSSACHS. SOMETIMES DESCRIBED AS 'THE HIGHLANDS IN MINIATURE', THE TROSSACHS ARE EASILY ACCESSIBLE FROM CENTRAL SCOTLAND, AND PROVIDE WONDERFUL OPPORTUNITIES FOR WALKING, CYCLING AND CANOEING.

CURLING, 'THE ROARING GAME', IS STILL ENORMOUSLY POPULAR IN SCOTLAND. RARELY, HOWEVER, DOES THE ICE BECOME THICK ENOUGH FOR AN OPEN-AIR MATCH, A 'BONSPIEL', LIKE THIS ONE ON THE LAKE OF MENTEITH.

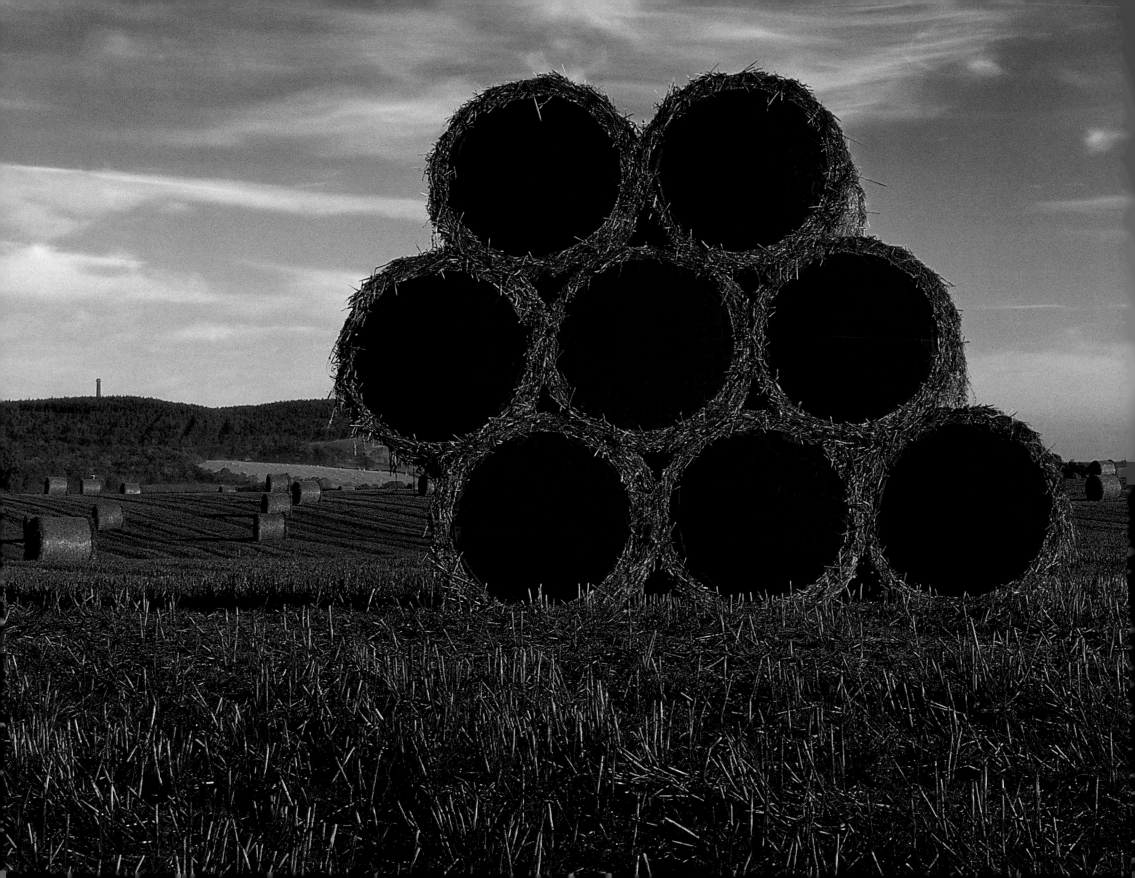

132

STIRLING'S FORMIDABLE CASTLE HAS HAD A CENTRAL PART TO PLAY IN THE POLITICS AND HISTORY OF SCOTLAND. MANY ARE THE KINGS AND ARMIES, SIEGES AND BATTLES IT HAS SEEN OVER THE CENTURIES.

OLD STIRLING BRIDGE HAS NOT REMAINED UNSCATHED DURING ITS 500 YEARS' EXISTENCE. ONCE IT
WAS PARTLY ROOFED; IN 1745 AN ARCH WAS REMOVED TO BLOCK THE ADVANCE OF THE JACOBITES.

PREVIOUS PAGE. IN RECENT YEARS TRADITIONAL STOOKS OF SHEAVES HAVE BEEN REPLACED BY HUGE ROUND BALES,
WHICH LOOK IMPRESSIVE IN A LANDSCAPE. THIS STRIKING WORK OF 'STRAW ART' WAS CREATED NEAR CUPAR, FIFE.

THROWING THE HAMMER AT THE STIRLING HIGHLAND GAMES. STIRLING MAY SEEM TO BE A STRANGE VENUE FOR A HIGHLAND GAMES, BUT THESE ARE HELD THROUGHOUT SCOTLAND, NOT EXCLUSIVELY IN THE HIGHLANDS.

OVERLEAF. THE CHIMNEYS AND COOLING-TOWERS OF GRANGEMOUTH, THE CENTRE OF SCOTLAND'S PETRO-CHEMICAL INDUSTRY AND ITS BUSIEST PORT, CREATE A FANTASTIC, FUTURISTIC LANDSCAPE IN CONTRAST TO THE SCENIC BEAUTY OF THE SURROUNDING COUNTRYSIDE.

135

THE WALLACE MONUMENT, OVERLOOKING THE FORTH VALLEY AND THE CLACKMANNANSHIRE HILLS, COMMEMORATES THE NATIONAL
HERO AND GREATEST OF ALL FIGHTERS FOR SCOTLAND'S INDEPENDENCE, SIR WILLIAM WALLACE.

THE UNMISTAKABLE ARCHES OF THE FORTH RAILWAY BRIDGE SEEN FROM NORTH QUEENSFERRY. COMPLETED IN 1890, IT REPLACED
A HAPHAZARD SYSTEM OF FERRIES SUCH AS THE ONES WHICH GAVE SOUTH QUEENSFERRY ITS NAME.

HARDY BATHERS TAKE TO THE FREEZING WATERS OF THE FORTH FOR THE NE'ER DAY DOOK. THIS TAKES PLACE

EVERY NEW YEAR'S DAY, AND PROVIDES A BRACING TONIC AFTER THE EXCESSES OF THE NIGHT BEFORE!

PREVIOUS PAGE. EDINBURGH CASTLE CROWNS ONE OF THE MOST FAMOUS SKYLINES IN THE WORLD. THE CASTLE SITS ON AN EXTINCT

VOLCANO AND HAS BEEN FORTIFIED SINCE THE IRON AGE. ITS HISTORY REFLECTS THE HISTORY OF SCOTLAND.

142

FOURTEENTH CENTURY CRICHTON CASTLE IN MIDLOTHIAN PASSED THROUGH MANY HANDS BEFORE BEING RENOVATED IN A FANTASTICAL RENAISSANCE STYLE BY FRANCIS STEWART,
5TH EARL OF BOTHWELL. THOUGH RUINOUS NOW, IT REMAINS A FASCINATING BUILDING.

THE CLIFFS OF BASS ROCK IN THE FORTH ARE WHITE WITH FLOCKS OF SEABIRDS, MOSTLY GANNETS. GEOLOGICALLY A
VOLCANIC PLUG, IT HAS A LIGHTHOUSE AND HAS BEEN USED AT TIMES AS A PRISON.

ANCIENT FOLK CUSTOMS SURVIVE IN SCOTLAND. IN THE BURRY MAN FESTIVAL OF SOUTH QUEENSFERRY, AN OBSCURE
PAGAN RITUAL, A LOCAL MAN IS COVERED IN BURRS (STICKY SEEDS) AND ESCORTED THROUGH THE STREETS.

INTO THIS BEAUTIFUL, FIFTEENTH-CENTURY CHURCH, ROSSLYN CHAPEL, MIDLOTHIAN, IS CRAMMED AN EXTRAORDINARY PROFUSION OF INTRICATE STONE CARVING.
ACCORDING TO TRADITION, THE HOLY GRAIL OF ARTHURIAN LEGEND IS CONCEALED WITHIN ITS WALLS.

THE EDINBURGH FESTIVAL, THE WORLD'S GREATEST ARTS FESTIVAL,
TAKES PLACE EVERY YEAR IN AUGUST. DURING A THREE-WEEK PERIOD, THOUSANDS OF
PERFORMANCES OF THEATRE, MUSIC, DANCE AND COMEDY TAKE PLACE IN BOTH THE OFFICIAL
AND FRINGE FESTIVALS. THE STREETS OF EDINBURGH ARE THRONGED WITH PERFORMERS,
EITHER PUBLICISING THEIR SHOWS OR JUST ENTERTAINING THE CROWDS OF
VISITORS WHO FLOCK TO THE CITY FROM AROUND THE WORLD.

THE FIREWORKS CONCERT AT THE END OF EVERY FESTIVAL IS ATTENDED BY HUGE CROWDS. AS AN ORCHESTRA PLAYS IN PRINCES STREET GARDENS,
A SPECTACULAR DISPLAY OF FIREWORKS ERUPTS FROM THE BATTLEMENTS OF EDINBURGH CASTLE.

FEW SCOTS HAVE HAD SUCH A PROFOUND EFFECT ON THEIR COUNTRY,
FOR GOOD OR ILL, AS JOHN KNOX (1513-72). THIS STATUE OF THE SCOTTISH REFORMATION'S
LEADING FIGURE STANDS OUTSIDE NEW COLLEGE, EDINBURGH.

A BAGPIPE MAKER TESTS A CHANTER IN HIS EDINBURGH WORKSHOP. THE PIPER BLOWS AIR INTO THE BAG AND SQUEEZES IT WITH HIS ELBOW THROUGH THE
CHANTER AND DRONES, CREATING THE INIMITABLE SKIRL OF THE PIPES.

PRINCES STREET, EDINBURGH'S MAIN SHOPPING STREET, HAS A MAGICAL AND FESTIVE AIR AT CHRISTMAS-TIME. ALWAYS THRONGED
WITH SHOPPERS, THE STREET FEELS OPEN AND SPACIOUS BECAUSE OF THE GARDENS RUNNING ALL ALONG ONE SIDE.

THE HOGMANAY (NEW YEAR'S EVE) PARTY IN EDINBURGH
IS ONE OF THE BIGGEST IN THE WORLD. AS FIREWORKS BURST IN THE CAPITAL,
AND A NEW MILLENNIUM BEGINS, ALL OF SCOTLAND CELEBRATES.